M000199906

AI
AS YOUR
TEAMMATE

AI
AS YOUR
TEAMMATE

**Electrify Growth
without Increasing Payroll**

EVAN RYAN

AI as Your Teammate

Electrify Growth without Increasing Payroll

ISBN 978-1-5445-2632-4 *Hardcover*
       978-1-5445-2630-0 *Paperback*
       978-1-5445-2631-7 *Ebook*

To the village it took to get here,

especially Annamarie, Carl,

Mom, and Dad.

Contents

1   Part 1

Understanding AI and its Potential

3   Introduction

17   Chapter 1

The Great Unknown that is AI

35   Chapter 2

AI is Boundless Leverage

67   Part 2

Using the AI Success Formula

69   Chapter 3

Getting Started with AI Today

91   Chapter 4

Automation 201: Custom Automations

109   Chapter 5
Build Your Project Team

135   Chapter 6
Your Team's Bigger Future after AI

145   **Conclusion**

149   **Further Resources**

Part 1

UNDERSTANDING AI AND ITS POTENTIAL

Introduction

I n 1996, IBM used its AI, Deep Blue, to compete against the world champion of chess, Garry Kasparov.

Researchers started development on what would become Deep Blue in 1985. Eleven years later, it was ready to play chess in prime time.

Kasparov beat Deep Blue four games to two. The IBM team went back to work.

Over the next fifteen months, Deep Blue received massive upgrades to its artificial intelligence logic. Deep Blue and Kasparov faced off again.

For the first time ever, an AI had beaten the best chess player in the world in a six-game rematch.

Fast forward to 2012: a company based out of England, called DeepMind, built an AI that could play most Atari games.

A key difference between this AI and the AI used in Deep Blue is that this AI was not taught any of the rules of the game or how the controls worked. It could "see" where the ball moved on the screen and if a brick was broken, but it had no other knowledge of the game, its rules, its controls, or its strategies.

It's simply told to acquire the highest score it can.

In this case, the AI was playing the game *Breakout*. It's like *Brick Breaker*, where there is a ball on the screen and little bricks at the top. The player's job is to use a slider at the bottom to make sure the ball hits all the bricks. Each time a brick is broken, your score increases. Each time you clear all the bricks on the screen, a new game starts, and the ball moves faster.

The first game begins, and the AI can't even move the slider that's at the bottom of the screen. It doesn't know controls for the slider exist! The ball fell from the middle of the screen to the bottom, the slider didn't move, and the game restarted.

Ten minutes after the AI began playing the game, it figured out that a slider exists and it can move, but the slider doesn't hit the ball often, if at all. That said, when the slider does hit the ball, the ball breaks a brick! The score increases, and the AI learns it was a step in the right direction.

After two hours, the AI plays like an expert. It reliably uses the slider to hit the ball and wins the game most of the time. Even if the ball is moving extremely fast, it can accurately predict where the ball will be by the time it reaches the slider. The AI breaks all the bricks.

The DeepMind team allowed the AI to keep playing, even after it figured out how to play like an expert.

After four hours of the AI playing the game nonstop, it figured out that the most optimal way to maximize the score on the screen was to not only eliminate all the bricks, but to do it by using as few slider hits as possible.

The AI discovered that a huge risk to losing the game is the slider hitting the ball. It makes sense, logically, because every time the ball falls to the slider, the slider could miss the ball and the game is over. *What if there was a way to win the game without risking the slider missing the ball?*

The AI had also discovered that the top wall of the screen, the wall where the bricks sit, bounces the ball back down. So, at the beginning of the game, the AI used the slider to eliminate the bricks on the far-left side of the screen against the wall, thereby digging a tunnel.

The AI hit the ball in such a way that the ball went through the tunnel, hit the back wall, hit a brick, bounced off the back wall, and did it again.

The AI started knocking out the bricks *by playing against the back wall*. The slider was only used a few more times.

2015.

DeepMind, now a subsidiary of Google, taught a computer how to play the game of *Go*. *Go* is a game where each player has a set of stones, and to win, you must use your stones to surround your opponent's stones on a board that has a grid structure like graph paper.

If you aren't familiar with the game, don't worry. Most details and strategies aren't integral to the story.

A detail that does matter is the level of complexity of the game. In any game of chess, after each player has taken five turns, the number of unique games that could have been played totals over 69 trillion. Specifically, it totals over 69,352,859,712,417 unique games.

In any game of *Go*, there are 1,000,000,000,000,000,000,0 00,000,000,000,000,**000,000,000,000,001** unique games. The bolded part of that number is over 13X the complexity of chess. *Go* is really, really complex. It is so complex, in fact, that there are more unique games of *Go* than there are atoms in the universe.

DeepMind taught their new *Go* algorithm, *AlphaGo*, the rules and strategies of the game by having the AI play against human players. Professional *Go* players would play on a screen against the computer, and with every move, the AI learned more and got better and better at the game.

AlphaGo was defeating professional players, so in March 2016, and watched by over 200 million people, *AlphaGo* played in a five-day tournament against Lee Sedol.

Lee is widely recognized as one of the most skilled *Go* players in the last one hundred years. He has dedicated his entire life to *Go*. Lee became a professional *Go* player at age twelve. He is a national hero to the people of South Korea, and he has won over fifteen world championships.

Several weeks prior to the March tournament against *AlphaGo*, Lee won a major Korean *Go* tournament. Heading into the first game against the AI, Lee predicted that he would win in a "landslide." It makes sense; Lee was a top-five player in the world, all-time.

The first game began, and Lee appeared to be in control. After 102 moves into the game, *AlphaGo* played a move that was described as "exquisite." It was so exquisite, in fact, that Lee pondered his next move for ten minutes. Lee was having a very different experience than the Korean *Go* tournament a few months prior.

AlphaGo won the first game.

In the second game, *AlphaGo* played a move that shocked Lee and the television broadcasters. It was a move that had never been played before. *AlphaGo* had a bug, and it showed on move number thirty-seven.

Unlike *Breakout*, where the objective is to "maximize the score on the screen," *AlphaGo*'s objective is to "maximize the probability of winning." It didn't matter if it was winning by one stone or by dozens. It just needed to win.

AlphaGo played by learning to understand the current placement of the stones on the board. On its turn, it would play out the rest of the moves of the game based off each of its possible moves in the present. It was playing the game hundreds, or thousands of times, with each move. It calculated, *"If I do this, Lee might do that, which would make me do this,"* for every scenario.

During the second game, the commenters couldn't tell who was ahead, but *AlphaGo* knew it had a high chance at winning. What about the bug at move thirty-seven?

AlphaGo determined that the particular move would not maximize its score. It would, however, prevent Lee from scoring later in the game. Toward the end, that's exactly what it proved to do. *AlphaGo* won the second game.

In the end, *AlphaGo* defeated Lee Sedol, the best player in a generation, four games to one.

None of this has any direct correlation with how you grow your business. I would venture to guess your business doesn't make money or support operations by playing games like chess, *Go*, or Atari *Breakout*.

So why start a book about AI with these stories?

Because I would also guess that most of your business processes aren't nearly as complicated as *Go*.

So you can get started with AI today.

Your next 10X jump will be driven by your current team and AI in collaboration.

Your next 10X jump in revenue, profit, and impact will be driven by your current team creating bigger value.

Right now, your current team is slammed. They can't create bigger value while they are stuck completing the same tasks day-in and day-out. The pathway to their bigger future, and the pathway to your next 10X jump, is AI.

Artificial intelligence completes tasks automatically without ever taking a vacation, sick day, or asking for a raise.

As you automate more and more tasks, your team becomes more and more free. At first, they save an extra five or ten minutes, but over time, automations save your team five hours per week. Then, ten hours. Then, twenty hours. Suddenly, your team has saved 500 or even 1,000 hours per year. What happens then?

In a future where AI is your teammate, AI elevates everyone in the company to create bigger value while doing more fascinating work. By performing dozens, or hundreds, of tasks per week that used to be done by your team, AI becomes the backbone of your company. It keeps the key operations running, 24/7.

Your team can be more creative than ever.

What new markets would they help you enter? What new business opportunities exist that you can't focus on yet because you're too busy in the present? What new products can you create? What new supply chain opportunities exist but you haven't had time to capitalize on?

These are the types of questions your team can answer when they have AI as their teammate.

The key to your bigger future is not that AI gives you, the entrepreneur, greater leverage. *It's that AI gives your team greater leverage.* The paradigm shift is enormous.

This book is for entrepreneurs who have ambition far greater than their current capabilities.

I have spoken with too many entrepreneurs who want to grow their business 10X, but they can't stand the thought of increasing the size of their team by 10X.

In the past, their entrepreneurial success was predicated on investing profit into new areas of their business, new talent, machines, and market segments. They've worked for years or decades to build the business to where it is, and the only thing that they know to be certain is that they don't want to slow down. Not only do they want to speed up, but they also want to speed up easier and cheaper than before.

I've worked with hundreds of entrepreneurs over the last several years. There's one giant commonality that has afflicted most of them. They want to grow without drastically increasing payroll. While they know AI is coming and could be a possible option for their business, they don't know where to start.

If you are someone who not only wants to discover where to start, but also wants to use AI to further your business, then this book is for you.

In this book, I'll take you through tools to think about AI as it affects your company. We will discuss what you need to know, what you don't need to know, and business transformations that come once AI is a member of your team.

Every business is unique. While we will dissect AI in both big-tech and low-tech businesses, we will show you how to find opportunities for AI specific to you.

We'll create clarity around the cost of AI projects of varying complexity. In Part 2, we will discuss how to hire an AI design and implementation team, including where you can cut costs and where you should invest more.

Lastly, and most importantly, we will discuss how your team can be elevated to create more fascinating and motivating value once AI is their teammate. We will address the future of your teamwork, and we will imagine the future of your business.

AI isn't being used in most small, non-tech businesses.

It's no secret that AI has been overpromised and underdelivered for the last few decades.

As of this writing, AI is actually beneficial: Google has saved 40 percent on their data center air conditioning expense because DeepMind (yes, the DeepMind that built *AlphaGo* and *AlphaGo Zero*) used AI to lower their cooling needs. Facebook's entire business, from newsfeed to ads, is AI. Tesla has cars that sort-of-self-drive, and most recently, Moderna and Pfizer used AI to develop the COVID-19 vaccine just three days after the virus's genome was sequenced.

AI isn't being used in most small, non-tech businesses.

Over the last several years, my company has coached hundreds of entrepreneurs on the transformations that can exist with AI, and we have built AI that has created millions of dollars in new value.

We launched businesses that became instant successes, turned nascent businesses into $0.00 marginal cost businesses overnight, helped serial entrepreneurs capture millions of dollars in new value, and we've helped new entrepreneurs get their businesses off the ground.

The next two chapters are about what AI is and what it means to a business. If you already understand these topics, feel free to move on to Part 2, where we dive into the formula for making any AI project successful, how to build your AI team, and how you can get started today.

TAKE ACTION!

The questions in the "Take Action!" section are the ones we most often ask our coaching clients. I recommend taking a minute or two and answering the questions on your phone or in this book.

We've put tons of resources on our book's website, ait.teammateai .com. In each chapter, I'll put a few of the resources that you can expect to find. All the resources on ait.teammateai.com are free.

1. What is your vision for your next 10X growth in business?

2. When was a time you experienced a creativity space? What was the result?

3. Who are some recent hires that transformed your business? What was their impact?

For more resources, videos of DeepMind's AI playing *Brick Breaker*, and links to a documentary about *AlphaGo*, head to ait.teammateai.com.

Chapter 1

THE GREAT UNKNOWN THAT IS AI

It's time to give your lazy data a task.

AI is data with a task.

A lot of businesses have a lot of data. There's data in spreadsheets, CRMs, ERPs, project management tools, emails, meetings, and dashboards. There's data in photos, videos, sales activities, audio, and PDFs.

Most of the time, this data sits idly as reference material if you're confused or conducting research. It's the laziest person on your team. Hopefully it is, anyway.

AI allows for all the data you have, in whatever form, to be put to work.

Who on your team orders the inputs to make your products? Who forecasts sales? Who does QA? Who is the handoff between your sales team and your customer success team?

What if your answer to all those questions above was *"an AI"*?

That is data with a task.

AI is like electricity.

There's an old Johnny Carson clip where he's interviewing the oldest farmer in Illinois. He asked the farmer, "What's the biggest change to farming since you started?"

"Electricity," said the farmer.

Think about the role electricity plays in your life now and think about what life would be like without it.

AI is like electricity. It permeates every industry. Yes, there are companies like mine and talented people that coach, build, and scale AI, but that can be compared to electric companies and electricians. Today, AI is the biggest change for every business in every industry.

What's the difference between AI and automation?

An AI purist will tell you that some of the simple automations contained in this book above are not AI. They'll say that if it's not a data-fed model, it's not AI; it's just software. I use the terms "AI" and "automation" interchangeably. If a task was once done by a human and is now done by a computer, who cares about the difference?

All the topics in this book are about how you can utilize computers and software as a teammate. We look to answer the question, *"How can you exponentially grow your business without increasing payroll?"* Whether it's true AI or automation, that starts with freeing up your team to do work that transforms your business faster, easier, cheaper, and bigger.

We've built complex AI and relatively simple automation. Oftentimes, businesses just need relatively simple automation, not letter-of-the-law AI.

I consider spirit-of-the-law AI to be any computer doing a task that was previously done by a human.

If you're an entrepreneur looking to exponentially grow your business without adding payroll, my guess is that you don't care about the difference between AI and automation. You care about growth and getting the job done. For that, the question I would ask myself is, "How could a computer do this for me?" or "How could a computer help my team work faster?"

We are looking to give your lazy, stagnant data a task.

Example: Hiring New Employees

Situation

Your company is hiring, which is great! Your company also spends too much time hiring, and you need a new way to create job postings, collect applications, organize them, review them, and schedule interviews.

Solution Exploration

There are many tools that already use AI to do everything except schedule interviews—Workday, ZipRecruiter, and Indeed, among many others.

For interview scheduling, it's easiest to simply add a Calendly link to the calendar of the person doing the phone screening. From there, the candidates will schedule their own interview times.

Nothing more is needed.

Example: Monitoring RFPs

Situation

You're a government contractor and you need to monitor the RFP and bid opportunities posted daily. This is an unbelievably boring job, and it's high turnover. Beyond that, it's time-consuming and, oftentimes, so mind-numbingly boring that there's a significant amount of human error.

In this case, the "data" is your process for identifying and finding new RFP opportunities. It's also the data on the web pages, which trigger the AI, currently the human, to alert the leadership of a new opportunity.

Solution Exploration

You set out to determine if a computer can monitor all the proper websites for you. Through your years of experience, you know certain keywords to look for and opportunities suitable for you. You don't need the AI to respond to the RFP, just alert you to it.

Solution Viability

You're looking for software to scrape certain websites and alert you to the opportunities that may fit your criteria. For the websites that don't allow scraping, you're looking for an RSS feed that you can run through the AI to determine, automatically, if the opportunity is right for you.

Solution Designer

Definitely hire a solution designer. This isn't an unbelievably intense project with the right leadership. Website scraping is a relatively common practice, but it can get expensive in a hurry if you don't have the right team in place.

The solution ends up being a combination of website scraping plus RSS feed analysis, which then runs through an AI which determines if the opportunity is right for you. All the right opportunities get emailed to you and the leadership team each morning.

Immediate Impact

You find way more opportunities than you'd found before. It ends up changing the game for you because you now can not only monitor all the government websites, but you can monitor other sites that host RFPs. Tons of RFP opportunities are miscategorized or addressed improperly, and you're able to respond to all of them. Beyond that, you no longer need to hire someone just to manage those opportunities. Now, you can hire a new individual to respond to RFPs and close new business.

Long-Term Impact

Over time, you build a whole system around this new AI, and it does most of your prospecting for you. You decide to build in some decision-making algorithms to help it even better determine the work you decide to do as well as the number of competitors you'll have, possibly even including the specific companies you'll be competing against. The days of having someone hired to do this work are long gone, and acquiring new business is more stable than ever.

All hype, or ready for prime time?

It's no secret that AI has been promised for decades and largely underdelivered. If you don't know how to use it, it would be easy to think it's underdelivering today.

In retrospect, most technology has seemed to be overhyped or to be underdelivering just until the point which it became ubiquitous. Let's examine a few decades.

The 1980s gave us the personal computer. They were limited in functionality, relatively difficult to use, and *very big*. Yet, Steve Jobs and Bill Gates positioned them as a technology as transformative as the printing press.

The 1990s gave us laptops and the internet. We may only remember technology in the ×90s as being useful, not as being "potentially unnecessary." Don't believe me? Head to YouTube and search "Today Show: What is the Internet Anyway?"

The early 2000s started with the dot-com bubble and ended with the iPhone. In the middle of the decade, when cell phones started to get cameras, Bill Maher, the comedian and host of *Real Time with Bill Maher*, opined, "It's a phone, not a Swiss Army Knife."

A primary complaint about the iPhone was that there was no keyboard. Personally, I remember many discussions with others expressing worry about how people just really liked clicking a key. They'll "mistype frequently," they're "faster with the T9 typing" (where button one is "ABC"), or they can "do everything on their computer."

In the end, Apple used AI to solve the problem for us. They had already built prototypes of the iPhone, but too many people were clicking the wrong buttons. According to Scott Forstall, the Apple executive overseeing the original iPhone OS software, the keyboard would (and still does) predict the next letters you'll type, and it changes the size of the "hit region," or the clickable area of the button, so you type more accurately.

Take the letter "t" for example. If you type it, there's a high likelihood you'll type an "h" next, because "the" is a very common word. Once the "t" is clicked, the "h" key becomes the "h," "g," and possibly some of the "b" and "y" keys, all without changing the way the "h" key looks to you. If you type the "h" key, the "e" key becomes huge, all without changing the way it looks to you.

In fact, Apple devices still do this today. Pay attention next time you get a new iPhone. I bet you'll have more typos than usual. The iPhone learns the way you type!

The 2010s brought us the cloud and actually beneficial AI. Self-driving cars, targeted ads, AI that can write copy, and AI that can even predict the folding of proteins. In the recent COVID-19 pandemic, AI was used to help sequence the genome of the COVID-19 virus and create the mRNA vaccine. All-in, from the time the genome was sequenced until we had the working version of the vaccine in phase one clinical trials, was three days.

Now, just like people expressed worry about the iPhone keyboard, business owners are expressing worry about how they "really just need a person to do the task."

AI in the 2020s will be like internet in the early 2000s.

The expressions, complaints, and pessimisms of the previous decades seem ridiculous today. Looking back, it's easy to connect the dots and say to yourself, "Of course the things that happened would happen."

But if I'm going to claim that AI in the 2020s will be like internet in the early 2000s, let's examine the claim with the dots we have now.

AI is all around you.

We live in a Zoom world, don't we?

It's hard to remember how bad video conference services were, but for most of the life of video conferencing, you could hardly see or hear people if the internet network was anything less than perfect. Zoom uses AI to compensate for network bandwidth issues and make the video and audio clear for everyone on the call.

Uber and Lyft use AI to determine who is going to pick you up and the route they'll use to get you to the destination.

Facebook and Twitter use AI to determine what content to show you next to keep you on the site as long as possible.

High-frequency traders use AI to predict where the market is headed in an effort to front-run the market by 1/1000 of a second, making billions of dollars per year.

But what about small businesses?

▸ Zapier, IFTTT, and Microsoft Flow help small businesses save hours and hours per week using simple automations.

▸ Engineering firms use AI for quality assurance to look at inspection videos and photos to make sure every product looks up to code.

▸ Newsrooms, even the small ones, use AI to write and publish news articles.

▸ Law firms use AI to automate the finding of relevant research and background information.

▸ Manufacturing companies use AI to determine their supply and resource needs of specific materials for procurement.

- Marketing agencies use AI for writing their marketing copy and for creating imagery design.

In the not-so-distant future:

- Companies will be able to create AI chatbots that actually create value (I tend to think they don't right now).

- They'll use AI for outbound sales and replace entire outbound prospecting teams.

- All procurement will be done by AI, and most budgeting, finance, and balancing will be done by AI.

- Most emails will be written by AI. Most marketing and sales copy will be written by AI.

- Contracts will be written by AI. Social media graphics will be created with AI, and videos will be voiced over by AI.

- Call centers will be staffed by AI. This means there will always be a zero-minute wait.

- Your administrative assistant will largely be replaced by AI. This will allow you to turn that individual into a strategic assistant.

- A great part of your product delivery, whatever your product is, will have an AI component.

This is much sooner than twenty years away. We've already built or used software that can do most of these tasks. You can either be on the forefront of adopting this technology, or you can wait a few more years. As Peter Diamandis, the founder of XPrize Foundation, likes to say, "In ten years, there will be two types of businesses. Those that use AI, and those that are out of business."

The pace of AI acceleration is accelerating.

From Harry Potter to the doctor

In 2019, an AI research company funded by Elon Musk, called OpenAI, released a language algorithm called GPT-2.

Language algorithms can be powerful. They generate the output text once given starter text. In the Harry Potter example, the starter text was the content of the first seven books, then its output was the first chapter of the eighth.

You'd recognize these algorithms better by the memes that started with something like, "I had an AI read all seven *Harry Potter* books, and it wrote the first chapter of the eighth book."

Most of these memes were humorous. The AI, of course, doesn't understand what it's writing; it just learns the style and characteristics of what it's read and writes character-by-character. Seriously, not even word-by-word, but character-by-character.

The AI knows of Harry and his friends, it knows of Voldemort as a character, it knows of magic, and it knows that Harry and his friends overcome obstacles, but it doesn't understand the nature of the obstacles, characters, or magic. If asked, "Why is it so important that Harry defeat Voldemort?" it would have no idea why. It can write, but it can't understand.

While these memes were funny, sometimes, the outputs are stunning.

Over three decades ago, a three-year-old by the name of Colin Megill was playing with his aunt. His aunt was swinging him around, and he felt a pop in his right shoulder.

As he grew up, he had difficulty gaining muscle mass on his right side. It was difficult for him to swim and keep up with his classmates. There were times where it was excruciatingly painful for him to do a task, like driving a stick shift vehicle.

Over the course of the next thirty-five years, Colin visited dozens of doctors and physical therapists. No one could figure out what was wrong with him. He ended up in the office of a surgeon who works with minor league baseball teams. The surgeon, having seen this before, gave him an MRI and correctly diagnosed him with a torn labrum. Shortly after, he had surgery, and his shoulder was fixed for good.

Fast forward to 2020.

OpenAI has updated their GPT-2 algorithm and released a new version they call GPT-3. Remember, it does language. So you can give the algorithm starter text, and it will write the rest of the sentence, paragraph, or blog post. It can write as much as it wants.

At a technical level, GPT-3 is 15X more sophisticated than GPT-2. You could have it read all seven *Harry Potter* books, and the first chapter of the eighth book *might actually be good.* Its outputs are incredible. People use GPT-3 for marketing copy, to write code, to write emails, and to even write entire blog posts. It can research, understand, and even complete spreadsheets. We've used it in production environments.

But not Colin Megill.

Colin, having already recovered from his surgery and now with strength in his right arm, typed the following starter text into GPT-3:

> "The child is having pain in his right shoulder. It is difficult to drive a stick shift, throw a ball, and lift his arm above his head to open cabinets. Moving heavy blankets off his body in the middle of the night is very painful, and the child is unable to develop muscle mass on his right shoulder or right bicep. The child is suffering from..."

GPT-3's response:

> "...a torn labrum. The doctor schedules him for surgery."

It took thirty-two years for doctors to diagnose Colin. It took one year for OpenAI to take an algorithm that was a meme, writing *Harry Potter*, and update it to the point where it was able to diagnose a medical condition.

And it was never intended for medicine.

This is not a statement on AI replacing doctors. I don't think that'll happen. This is a statement on how the usability of AI is accelerating. If an AI that was writing humorous, but bad, *Harry Potter* chapters one year ago can now correctly diagnose a medical issue, how could an AI help you?

Could AI help you forecast sales better? Could it help you spend less on inventory? Process RFPs faster? Could it help you automate 50 percent of your team's time in the customer fulfillment process, thereby reducing order fulfillment for your clients?

Could it lower your costs so much that your clients become your competitors?

If you are uninterested, retiring soon, or resistant to the change, the rest of this book is not for you. I hope you gift it to a friend.

The pace of AI is accelerating, and it's ready for prime time.

TAKE ACTION!

1. What are some examples of data in your business?

2. What do you know about AI now that you didn't know before?

3. When was the last time you were surprised by the usefulness of technology?

For more examples of data, further info about AI and how it works, that hysterical clip of the farmer on Johnny Carson, and more, head to ait.teammateai.com.

Chapter 2

AI IS BOUNDLESS LEVERAGE

The ancient Egyptians could have built the pyramids by forcing a lot of people to carry the heavy stones up the pyramid steps, or they could pull stones up ramps and build the pyramids much faster. At that time, simple technology, such as a ramp, was an excellent form of leverage. Now, we have new technology.

The key mindset for adopting AI, for you and for your team, is *leverage*. For your team, AI is a form of leverage that allows them to create more fascinating and motivating value. It's a way for them to increase their value to the company and build new skillsets. For you, it's a way to create even greater systemization, repeatability, scale, and reliability in your business.

It's a way for you to exponentially grow your business without adding payroll.

From old world leverage to new world leverage.

As a successful entrepreneur, you've already used many types of leverage to get you to this point. You've used capital leverage (cash) to grow the business. Maybe you used capital leverage to buy labor leverage, hiring an employee or contractor. That employee may be a highly creative person who gave you the opportunity to create content like a podcast, social media post, or blog. That content leverage helped you grow as more people consumed it and became familiar with your brand. That contractor could've been a developer who writes code (technology leverage) or a CNC machine operator (labor leverage and technology leverage) who scales your output.

At some point, you built a website (technology leverage). That website allowed you to attract new clients.

You've successfully utilized leverage to grow your business before. This chapter is about the mindset transition from old world leverage to new world leverage.

Old world leverage is finite leverage like cash and labor. You can run out of cash, and you can run out of labor.

New world leverage, such as technology and creativity, is boundless. Writing code and being creative don't cost any money.

Your future growth is based on successfully implementing new world leverage.

We live in a world where any problem that can be solved with software, which is virtually any problem that is solved on a screen, is solvable. Combined with advanced robotics, which are closer than they seem, we are living in a world where virtually any problem, whether made up of atoms and elements or bits and bytes, can be either completely solved or aided by technology.

The shortage is not the technological capabilities. The shortage is creativity in problem solving.

Creativity is new world leverage because there is no upper limit to its potential. Whether it's in solving problems or creating possibilities, there's always more room for creativity.

All new breakthroughs in your business are the result of someone's creativity.

Creativity, itself, is not new. Its boundlessness comes from technology's ability to turn your idea into reality.

You can have a robot kitchen, a robot vacuum, and a car that drives itself. You can have an AI design your clothes, a robot manufacture your clothes, and a robot fold them for you once they're clean. You can dream an entirely new universe in *Minecraft*.

Before advanced technology, creativity was limited to the physical world of atoms and elements. Now, with advanced technology, creativity is unlimited through bits and bytes.

Your business has most likely already started to implement this new world leverage. The easiest examples are instant communication, video conferencing, and file storage.

Instant communication tools like Slack have allowed your team to iterate faster, answer questions quickly, and eliminate a lot of dead space that is created when there's a knowledge gap.

Video conferencing tools like Zoom allow your team to take a face-to-face meeting anywhere with full screenshare capabilities. As long as you have internet access, your business continues to run.

File storage tools like Dropbox allow your team to share files instantly. Gone are the days where you needed to walk a piece of paper or a folder over to a coworker's desk. Now, you can send a link, and the file has been shared.

These types of tools may seem rudimentary, but they're truly incredible forms of new world leverage.

First, they increase your team's productivity greatly. Your team can get work done much faster and more easily. For you, that means you just received the same output faster and cheaper.

Think about how annoying it used to be when a file was lost, and it took someone an entire morning, or longer, to find it. Remember when a project would be stalled for an entire day because a coworker couldn't answer a quick question without being in person?

Think about the amount of time spent in airports and on airplanes traveling to in-person presentations. Now, a significant percentage of those meetings can take place over Zoom.

Second, these tools increase your team's flexibility. With these three tools, your team can be fully remote, all the time. My team has been fully remote since day one, and the foundation of our business was built on these three capabilities.

These tools change your labor leverage needs. Now, you don't need to hire someone in the same location to complete a job because it's all online. You can hire someone from another state or country who's either more qualified, cheaper, or both. This changes your cash position because you can get much more bang for your buck.

But what does any of this have to do with AI?

I leveraged several forms of technology in writing this book. In fact, I used so much AI in writing this book, I was able to write the entire first version of the manuscript, complete with the first nine rounds of edits, in five weeks. All while I ran my business.

I knew the topic. That part was easy. I wanted to transform the reader's thinking from "I know AI is coming, but I don't know where to start" to "I know what it is, how we can use it, how to build an AI team, how much it'll cost, and how my current team will create bigger value in the future."

Next, I created an outline. This was done completely by me. What were the eight to ten big topics I wanted to cover? What were the most common questions I receive from prospects and clients? These are questions like, "What can't AI do?" and "How much does AI cost?" and "What talent do I need on my team?"

Then, I asked people to interview me. All I gave them was the outline and told them to ask good questions.

Then, the AI stepped in.

We recorded the interviews using Zoom and used an AI transcription service to turn the interviews into text.

I took all the interview text and grouped it together in the same order as the outline. I did a once-over removing any interludes, like "I need to explain this idea more clearly" or "This idea doesn't fit in this section," and I created a working manuscript.

V0.1 complete.

I think the worst part of writing a book has got to be staring at your blinking cursor with no words written. By using the interviews and AI transcription, I avoided that and had a working manuscript.

I spent the rest of my time editing.

I made things sound less like I was informally saying the content and more like I had written the content. I would add some sections and remove others. I edited for conciseness and clarity.

All of this was editing, though, not writing. There's a huge difference between being an author and being a typer. I want to be the former. In this case, the AI was my typer. It's much faster this way.

This is technology leverage. It's leverage that allows you to accomplish more, faster.

Technology leverage, defined.

Technology leverage is using technology to keep aspects of your business optimized and running without human intervention.

You enhance your business's current capabilities through technology. Websites, Zoom, Slack, and Dropbox are all examples of this.

For the price of a subscription, you can drastically enhance your team's workflow. You can buy access to all sorts of tools that make your workday easier.

You've used technology leverage before.

This isn't your first rodeo.

Remember the time before email? Fax. Remember the time before fax? Snail mail.

What feels natural now was not always the case.

There was a time when you mailed contracts. Then, fax came along and made it much easier to send paper documents. Then, email came, and you could send the document digitally. Then, Dropbox came, and you could provide access to a document of any size or type.

Before CRMs, people used a Rolodex. Your sales team would have pieces of paper with important client information, and they would make phone calls using that paper. If you lost the salesperson, you lost those contacts. Now, you have a CRM that's based on the internet—if you lose the salesperson, you keep the contacts. If your office catches on fire, you don't lose all your prospects. If you want to measure sales activities like the number of outbound reach-outs per week, you can do so at the click of a button.

Before, targeted and programmatic ads were billboards, street benches, and radio. You advertised in a location and hoped that the right individual would see your ad. That said, you had no idea how many people would see it, who they were, what their demographics were, or if the ad converted. Now, you can see the exact number of people who see your ads, the ads can be targeted by demographic, and often, the ad is tailored to reach someone who needs your solution *but doesn't know it yet.*

Before, ERP solutions were spreadsheets full of inventory lists and pick lists. Before that, there were paper pick lists. If that list was misplaced, you had to rely on someone with institutional knowledge of your products to remake the list. If that person wasn't in the office that day or suddenly quit, the job didn't get done.

You and your team are familiar with technology leverage. You've used technology to save your team time and energy before. AI is a greater extension of that, where instead of providing your team faster ways of completing the same task, you're providing your team with a way to not do the task at all, yet the task still gets done. Toward the end of Part 2, we'll explore what your team can do with all the extra free time they'll have because of technology leverage.

Owned technology is a game changer.

While most businesses buy licenses and subscriptions, they never consider owning technology.

The nature of owned technology leverage is that it has high fixed cost and $0.00 marginal cost. That means that you build it once and use it repeatedly. Or you build it once and sell it repeatedly.

Facebook built the Newsfeed product once. They sell ad space on it over and over repeatedly. Dropbox, Slack, and Zoom built their services once and sold it repeatedly.

You can build an AI that you pay for once and utilize repeatedly. Let me give you an example.

We have a company named Lede AI in partnership with a news-paper called Richland Source. In this company, an AI writes and publishes sports stories without any human intervention. Our AI has written and published hundreds of thousands of newspaper articles.

We built the AI one time over the course of several months at a very high cost. Because our cost to write the code was very high, the cost to write the first article was the same as the cost to write the algorithms. Think about it, the first article cost the same as the cost of the entire development!

The second article was written. This decreased the cost per article to 50 percent of the development cost.

The third article was written. The cost per article was now 33 percent of the development cost.

There is zero marginal cost to write the articles, so with each new article our AI wrote, the cost per article continued to further decrease.

Lede AI is a newswire, and we have media outlets all over the country that subscribe to receive our content. Each time we send them content, it costs us effectively nothing to write the content, since the code to write and publish articles was already written years ago. We make money from our clients with effectively no cost of goods sold!

Example: Sales Forecasting

Situation

You own a retail company that's always struggled to accurately forecast sales. If you were asked "What keeps you up at night?" one of your top answers would be related to the revenue you'll bring in next quarter. You have lots of data over your years in business, but you don't know how to put it to good use without some of your calculations including "hope" as a strategy. You know hope isn't a strategy, but you don't know how to get more clarity.

Solution Exploration

You need to search to gather data, so you sit down with your team to determine which datapoints matter most. A few you come up with are the following:

- ▶ Median income of the community

- ▶ Number of households in the community

- ▶ If the store is on a street corner

- ▶ Number of parking spaces available

- ▶ Average cart value

- ▶ Average time in store

You're able to go back and gather that data, so a few weeks later, you've got all the data you think you need. You hire a solution designer, and they tell you to start with the AI, and if the AI can nail your sales forecasts, you don't need an application to start, but you may need one as you scale.

Solution Viability

The AI researcher cleans the data and runs it through several algorithms. A week or two later, they've brought you forecasts based off previous data. Assume, right now, it's Q4. They went back to a-year-ago-Q2 (twenty-one months ago) and looked to predict a-year-ago-Q3 (eighteen months ago). They were 80 percent accurate on their predictions, and they don't think they can get any better without more data.

Your solution designer does more research and finds an AI and dataset that predicts the price of items at auction with approximately 90-percent accuracy. That's way better than the 80 percent you're currently getting and will drive tons of decision making for the next month or quarter. Your solution designer starts modeling your dataset off the auction dataset as much as they can. It's not a perfect match, but it could get your sales forecast AI to be much closer. What started as one giant project now becomes two projects.

Project one: get all the data you can that is like the auction dataset (ninety days)

Project two: turn all that data into sales forecasts

Project one is helpful because it gets your team's data organized. Now, your team can begin measuring more and more metrics that you deem valuable toward better forecasting. Project two pays the bills (for now).

Solution Designer

Hired.

Immediate Impact

Your company starts nailing their sales forecasts. There's less waste and more clarity surrounding future financials and customer growth. Profitability increases sizably. You dive into a data gathering campaign to create *dials*.

In software, dials are cause-and-effect changes. You know that the current change in your results is because of the change you made. Think about the Facebook algorithm. It's got tons of dials. It can dial up your business page's organic reach or dial it down if it thinks you'll spend money on ads. It can dial up the number of ads it shows you as a consumer if it knows you're happy to scroll by or click ads, or it can dial them down if you're finicky about ads. It can dial up the amount of political content it shows you, and it can dial it down.

You find out more key metrics that drive sales, and, more importantly, you start A/B testing your locations to determine how particular sales, initiatives, and even signage drives change in your sales metrics. In your business, sales become a formula.

Long-Term Impact

Your competitors need the same data that you need, and you decide to create a division that helps businesses in similar industries better forecast their sales. Your financial research determines that it'll *increase* your margins while *decreasing your business risk*. Besides, with sales now working as a formula, your key talent is looking for something new to do.

Key team members become billable resources. After all, they need to help the businesses gather the data that you gathered in project one. As they're working as consultants, your application development team turns your sales forecasting solution into a software as a service (SaaS) platform. Then, you charge a subscription on your sales forecasting algorithm to the companies you just sold the solution to. Now, not only are you crushing it in your existing core business, but you've leveraged talent you hired to drive new revenue, you've leveraged technology you built to drive high-margin recurring revenue, and you've mitigated your retail business risk all at the same time.

The economics of new world leverage.

Imagine you had an AI that saved an employee five hours of work per week. Five hours, automated.

Each employee would save 250 hours per year. That's 12.5 percent of their year!

Assume you paid $10,000 to have that AI built and deployed.

If you pay that employee $60,000 per year in base salary, their hourly rate is $30.00 per hour. So, 250 hours saved multiplied by $30 per hour equals $7,500 savings right there. You've almost returned your entire investment in one year, not including any additional value that employee created.

Now let's say you have five employees who all save five hours per week using that AI.

Each employee you hire is a medium fixed cost, due to upstart time and training, but high marginal cost. Contrast that to owned technology leverage, which is a high fixed cost, but $0.00 marginal cost.

You spent the same $10,000, but you saved each of those five employees 250 hours per year. Now, instead of saving $7,500, you saved $37,500. You saved $7,500 per year for each employee!

In your first year, your ROI will be almost 4X!

Now, your employees can focus on new forms of value creation. They can bring in new revenue, find new markets, create new products, and find ways to cut expenses. That can turn your $37,500 savings into hundreds of thousands, or millions of dollars in new opportunities.

Next year, you save the same $37,500, but with no additional expenses.

The year after that, you save the same $37,500 with no additional expenses.

And so on.

When I first started my business, I was, like all new entrepreneurs, cash-strapped. I needed an assistant but couldn't afford one. I was caught in the trap of being too busy to be a one-person show, but too underfunded to hire employee number one.

My real need, then, was not new capabilities—although I certainly needed more skillsets—it was time. I needed an extra 50 percent of my week back. So I started researching: what if I could save twenty hours per week using automation?

Sure enough, I was able to find an AI that would keep me on track in my days, an AI that would send emails, an AI that would schedule tweets, and an AI that would add new Stripe customers to my mailing list. I figured out how to save Zoom videos to the cloud for free instead of paying $400.00 per year (At that stage, saving $400 was crucial!). These were the tip of the iceberg. After a few months, I'd found so many little AIs to help me that I had saved twenty hours per week.

Because of the twenty hours per week I got back, essentially for free, I closed a few more deals. Because of those deals, I was able to make my first hire. Within six months of having all those automations in place, my team grew from just me, to five people. Thanks to technology leverage saving me half my week, I was able to quintuple the size of my team.

Two quarters after making those hires, we had our best quarter yet. Our monthly revenues and number of clients more than doubled.

New world leverage is about your team.

What's the opportunity cost of high-value team members performing low-value tasks?

Technology leverage is intended to give you the opportunity to better utilize your right-fit team members and find wrong-fit team members a better fit.

You'll be the person who sees the profit at the end of the day, but it's about the team. Technology leverage is about allowing your team to make themselves replaceable so they can create the value that makes them irreplaceable.

Administrative assistants all over the globe used to perform only file management. Now, they can accomplish so much more because Dropbox replaces entire file storage rooms.

Entire companies were built around installing and maintaining phone systems inside of companies. Now, those companies can manage IT staffing and consulting around Zoom, voice-over-IP, and cybersecurity.

Your team spends too much time completing tasks that must be done but return too little. *What if they didn't need to be the person performing those tasks?*

Provide a leverage budget.

I want my team to make themselves more efficient.

One trick I use to make it easy to give my team leverage is by giving them a leverage budget of $150 per month per tool. If they believe something will make them faster and more efficient, they can buy that tool on the corporate card, no questions asked.

$150.00 per month seems like a lot, but if a tool saves a team member one hour per week, it's already paid for itself. Secondly, most productivity tools only cost about $30.00 per month, so I incentivize them to utilize the leverage and find a quality product without fearing it will be over budget.

That led to the greatest teamwork-based leverage ROI opportunity in our company's history.

I had no interest in hiring a full-time individual for testing software. We needed one, but I didn't want to hire for it because they're expensive, and they are a recurring cost I didn't want to absorb. The industry-standard wage for this individual would start at a $60,000 per year base.

I kept thinking, "There's got to be a better way to test."

In the meantime, it was on me and my development team to test the software before each release.

We became frustrated because the testing didn't feel like the best use of our time. That said, releasing untested software is *always* a bad idea. It is likely software bugs will slip into the real world.

But I gave my team a $150 per-tool per-month leverage. Cash leverage.

Several months went by and a member of my development team found a tool to perform automated software testing. Automated testing isn't a new concept, but this specific tool performs it in a way that allows us to input all possible testing scenarios and it will accurately test for those scenarios on our behalf. Automatically.

The only caveat was that it would take an additional several hours of development time per major release for us to account for all the test scenarios. So a little extra development time, but it could complete automated tests.

The price of this subscription? Just $30.00 per month.

The price of the additional development hours? About $1,000 per month.

My annual expense in software testing? Only $12,360.00 per year.

My annual savings on a software testing individual? Over $47,000 per year, not including benefits, hiring, firing, training, vacation, and management time.

Employee morale increased because we didn't need to test our software using humans anymore. Lastly, since we started utilizing automated testing, our reliability increased dramatically. Our customer satisfaction rating is the highest it's ever been.

And, with every new bug we find, we fix it, write our test case, and it's automated forever.

Using Lede AI as team leverage.

A full year after Lede AI wrote its first article, our partner, Richland Source, which is a local newsroom in Ohio, was gearing up for the first week of the high school football season.

Richland Source had a problem. Every football team wanted to be featured in the paper, but there were ten games that needed coverage. To be featured, an article needed photos from the game as well as quotes about how the game progressed. Lede

AI's articles are relatively informational. Because the AI isn't at the game, we don't know some details about the game. For example, we don't know what the crowd's reaction would be throughout each game. Richland Source only had three sports reporters. They decided to use Lede AI as their fourth journalist.

They sent their reporters to the first half of one game and the second half of another game. Six games passed. For the four games where the Richland Source reporters weren't present, they gave a few skilled fans field passes to take photos for the articles on the field. After the games, the reporters called the coaches for reactions. Then, around 10:30 p.m., the reporters began writing their feature stories.

They didn't start from a blank slate, however. Lede AI published our version of the story first and marked it as "developing." In minutes, the Lede AI stories were number one on Google search for all relevant search terms and were driving traffic to Richland Source's website.

Our competitor newspapers hadn't even published, and we were receiving page views and number one search rankings on Google.

The reporters finished up their stories, added the photos, and adjusted the developing Lede AI articles to fit their stories. We were already the top Google search result, and now we had the highest quality content to go along with it.

Richland Source had never done something like that before. The reader feedback was incredible.

Several months later, it was time for the statewide high school football championships. Again, there were too many games and not enough reporters. Richland Source used the same strategy as the first week of the season. The reporter, Curt, used the "developing" Lede AI story to take the top spot on Google search, providing immediate results for anyone looking for the scores in the current moment. Later, photography, quotes, fan reactions, and more were wrapped into the already-published article.

Eight months after that state championship game, I received a phone call from the editor of Richland Source. The state championship article started by Lede AI and updated by the journalist had won an excellence in journalism award. It beat newspapers of record such as the Columbus Dispatch and the Cleveland Plain-Dealer.

That's AI as your teammate.

A few years ago, a machine-human collaboration like this would've never been possible. Now, technology as a teammate can help employees create far bigger value in far less time.

But how do you know if an automation opportunity is worth pursuing? How do you know what can even be automated? Later in Part 2, I'll show you a formula for how you can design, risk-assess, price, and develop AI in any context. Coming up next, I will show you how to find ways to bring AI into your business and how you can get started today.

Example: Ecommerce

Situation

You run a very large ecommerce store that processes tens of thousands of transactions per day. Your advantage is having the largest variety of products of any of your competitors. You have over 70,000 SKUs, and you add and remove products from your website daily.

Your largest issue with this process is writing product descriptions that sell. It's become tiresome and boring to write the same descriptions repeatedly, and your team dreads the three to four hours they spend creating new descriptions for one hundred new SKUs each day. The descriptions have suffered, and therefore sales have suffered.

Solution Exploration

There are two real options in front of you. The first is hiring a few copywriters each day on Fiverr. This is an okay option but requires lots of management. Plus, Fiverr fees will start to add up over time.

The second is AI. Tools like CopySmith.AI and Copy.AI have the capability to write product descriptions. That would cost over $100 per month, and maybe over $1,000 per month, but it seems reasonable enough.

Solution Viability

You try out CopySmith.AI and Copy.AI to see if the adjusted workflow will work, and it looks like it will! Your team types in the product name and a few words about it, then, "click!" The AI returns sample product descriptions, and your team copies and pastes.

Solution Designer

Problem already solved and no solution designer is needed.

Immediate Impact

Your team has turned a three- to four-hour job into a thirty-minute job, and your turnover declined. Your sales start to rebound, and employee morale increases.

Long-Term Impact

The marketing team that was spending time (or not spending time) writing product descriptions can now focus on new ways to drive website traffic, and both CopySmith.AI and Copy.AI write blog posts automatically. The product marketing team transitions to the content marketing team, and a new SEO initiative begins. Over time, your search ranking on the major search engines increases to the top page for many of your SKUs, and your customer acquisition cost reflects it.

Example: Social Media Marketing/SEO Optimization

Situation

Your social media and content marketing team are the same team. You'd like to expand your digital presence, but the team is overwhelmed. Leadership is frustrated by algorithm changes from Facebook/Google and the amount of time it takes to drive actionable results. Your team is frustrated because they must choose between publishing more content at a lower quality or publishing a small amount of high-quality content.

Solution Exploration

Not splitting the difference between output and quality, you'd like to have your team publish lots of high-quality content. The solution is easy. You can use CopySmith.AI or Copy.AI to write all your first-draft copy.

Solution Viability

Your team starts using the free trial of one of the above services. It may not be perfect, but it's better than starting from scratch. The most important outputs are the blog post and social media caption outputs. Now, instead of ideating and typing blog posts, your team simply edits them. The time to publish a blog post is reduced by over 75 percent. Your social media captions retain the same high quality, but again, your team is only editing and not creating. The AI did the creative work.

Solution Designer

None needed.

Immediate Impact

Because your publishing needs are being met over 50 percent faster than they were before, your team begins creating more educational content to fill a market void. Your team is posting twice as much as they did before, but the new content, the educational content, drives tons of engagement. Your audience is still seeing what you need them to see, but the new content is bringing a new audience and converting the old audience into prospects.

Long-Term Impact

Quickly, your content marketing team becomes both top-of-funnel lead generation and existing customer retention. The content team expands into podcasts and more regular, long-form video content, and you find that you are a standout in the market, dominating all digital channels.

TAKE ACTION!

1. What are some of your most successful experiences using leverage?

2. What is the most useful technology leverage in your business?

3. What are some examples of your team fully utilizing different forms of leverage?

4. Would you ever own your own technology?

5. What do you think about $0.00 marginal cost businesses?

For more free resources about different forms of leverage, a write-up about the economics of $0.00 marginal cost businesses, and more head to ait.teammateai.com.

Part 2

USING THE AI SUCCESS FORMULA

Chapter 3

GETTING STARTED WITH AI TODAY

Find your guinea pig.

Most search queries of "AI for small business" return suggestions like "put a chatbot on your website" and "strengthen your cybersecurity with AI." Another small fraction of articles suggests you "start by understanding your data" and "know your bottlenecks."

There isn't much useful information for getting started with AI *right now*. AI is more than chatbots and cybersecurity, and getting started by "understanding your data" and "discovering bottlenecks" sounds like a recipe for lots of meetings that never go anywhere.

In this chapter, we will dive into concrete examples of how your business can utilize AI immediately. We will be discussing how using automation tools such as Zapier, IFTTT, or Microsoft Flow allow you to automate anything from small tasks to entire business processes without any code.

By the end of this chapter, you'll know how to discover opportunities and create automations to save *tons* of time (and I mean *tons* of time) without writing any code, including a playbook for how to get your team involved.

Zapier

Software-as-a-service (SaaS) platforms are ubiquitous today. These are any services where one can pay a monthly fee, then access the service readily over the internet. You use SaaS platforms all the time. Email; QuickBooks; file storage, such as Dropbox; communication platforms like Slack or Teams; Zoom; payment processing, such as Stripe; CRMs, like Pipedrive and Salesforce; and project management tools, like Asana or Trello, among thousands of other tools, are all examples of SaaS programs.

SaaS platforms have been nothing short of transformative. Take a file storage tool, such as Dropbox, as an example. Before

Dropbox, everything was on paper. There were storage rooms full of file boxes and organization codes to find every single paper in the room. If a coworker misplaced a file, it was a wild goose chase to find the original. Then, Dropbox came along and released online file storage and sharing via the cloud. Now, you can access any of your files from anywhere in the world at any time!

Think about your processes now. *How many of your or your employees' tasks require taking data from one SaaS platform and doing something with it in another?*

Allow me to provide a few examples:

▸ When a new customer signs up, send them an email.

▸ When a verbal agreement is reached with a prospect, send a contract.

▸ Turn TypeForm responses into a pivot table for data analysis.

▸ Add a new customer into QuickBooks.

▸ Post marketing email copy on LinkedIn.

- Transcribe a video and add captions.

- Add a Zoom link to your calendar invites.

- Add new customers to your email list.

Instead of your employees taking your data from one platform and doing something with it in another, what if a computer did it for you? How would they talk to each other?

Enter: the API. APIs allow different pieces of software to talk to each other.

Imagine you're at a restaurant. An API acts like the waiter, shuffling your order between you and the kitchen. All it does is carry information. An API allows SaaS platform A to talk to SaaS platform B.

Zapier allows you connect SaaS platforms together using an API to give your data a task. You can tell the platform, "If something happens in platform X, do an action in platform Y."

- "If I mark a new deal as "won" in my CRM, set up a new project in my project management platform."

- ▸ "If a new customer signs up for our service in Square, add them to our email list in MailChimp."

- ▸ "If I send a calendar invitation in Outlook, add my Zoom link."

- ▸ "If someone submits a TypeForm questionnaire, add their data into an Excel spreadsheet."

There are tons of tasks your team can automate in this way, but how can you automate processes that are unique to your business?

Activity Log

The first step in automating any task is knowing what tasks consistently need to be completed.

I recommend having your team keep a log of their job routine. On an Excel spreadsheet, have the individual create five columns:

1. Task

2. Why did you do it?

3. Amount of time the task took to complete

4. On a scale of one-to-five, where one means "I hated every second of this" and five means "I really enjoyed this task," rank your satisfaction with the task.

5. Number of times that task occurred this week

The number of times the task occurred in a week is an important metric. Imagine a task takes five minutes, occurs twelve times per week, and is relatively easy to automate. This automation would save an employee one hour per week, or over an entire work week per year. That automation saves a ton of time and may move up the priority list. On the flip side, if a task takes twenty-five minutes, occurs once per week, and is relatively difficult to automate, it may not be high on the priority list.

When calculating time spent on a task, it's important to address task switching penalties. These are hidden time wasters that cannot be excluded from the value of the automation. If a task is automated, there's also no task switching penalty. My recommendation is to multiply the amount of time a task usually takes by 1.33. If a task takes ten minutes, assume it was thirteen minutes. We often find that task switching penalties are enough, on their own, to pay for automations.

We've gotten pushback on the activity log before citing reasons like "micromanagement" and an employee being "too busy," but the reality is that you can't help them do more fascinating and motivating work if you can't help them automate the boring and mundane.

If automation becomes a change management challenge, you may want to consider starting with one employee who is open to change and willing to experiment. Typically, young people are good guinea pigs for this because they have a particularly strong hatred for boring tasks. Convincing young people to "just try it" so they can spend less time completing boring work is an easy sell.

From there, you can use that employee's progress as an example to the rest of your team as to why they should prioritize the activity log.

Trigger/Action

Each Zapier automation has two components: a trigger and an action.

The trigger is the starting gun for the automation. When the trigger is activated, the automation runs. The action is the automation, itself. Remember, your data is the laziest employee you have, and this is where you give it a task.

In the activity log, the trigger is the question, "Why did you do this task?" and the action is "What did you do?"

So, if a line in the activity log reads:

Task	Why	Time	1-5 Scale	# Occurrences/ Week
Sent email to a new customer.	Sending kickoff emails to new customers is part of our onboard process.	7 minutes	3	3

The trigger is "new customer created." In Zapier, find the service payment processing service. This could be Stripe, PayPal, Square, or most other comparable payment processors.

Your action is "send an email." Zapier accommodates for Gmail, Outlook, MailChimp, or any other email service. Send the message to the email address the client used to sign up for your service and use the first name on the payment processor to directly address the email recipient, then add the body copy.

Structurally, in Zapier, this looks like:

TRIGGER: In Stripe, when a new customer is created

ACTION: Use Outlook to send an email (*this is your welcome email*)

If a row in the activity log looked like this:

Task	Why	Time	1-5 Scale	# Occurrences/ Week
Sent invoice to new customer.	That's what we do after signing a contract.	10 minutes	2	2

Your automation would look like this:

TRIGGER: a DocuSign document is signed.

ACTION: using QuickBooks, create and send an invoice to the email address of the person who signed the DocuSign document.

Imagine you use Slack for communication and Stripe for payment processing. Let's say your team sends a personal note to each new customer thanking them for doing business with you. *But how do you know when you get a new customer?* You could connect Slack and Stripe using Zapier to receive a Slack message every time a new customer is created in Stripe.

TRIGGER: in Stripe, a new customer is created.

ACTION: send a Slack message to the customer fulfillment team.

Consider for a moment that you are the individual who writes the thank you notes.

Currently, they check Stripe to see if any new customers sign up each day. That means they logged into Stripe, they navigated to the "customers" section, and they checked the list. If there's a new customer (and there's only sometimes a new customer), they copy the email address, open their email, paste the address into their email "To:" spot, add a subject line, type the email, and press send.

Let's say that task takes twelve minutes. Five minutes to check to see if there's a new customer, and seven minutes to get the email sent. Accounting for task switching penalties, it takes fifteen minutes.

What if we could save those fifteen minutes?

Your employee's activity inventory looks something like this:

Task	Why	Time	1-5 Scale	# Occurrences/ Week
Check Stripe to see if we have any new clients.	We do this every day.	5 minutes	2	5
Send the client a thank you email.	We had a new client today.	7 minutes	2	2

TRIGGER: a new client is created in Stripe.

ACTION: use Outlook to send an email to the new client.

This automation would save that employee fifteen minutes. Let's also assume the employee checks new client data every day. Now, they just saved seventy-five minutes per week.

This savings, times fifty working weeks per year, means your employee just got over a week and a half back!

What if you discovered that your customer retention increased by 50 percent by sending *another* personalized note to this new client a few weeks later? You could add to your automation!

Your automation would now look like this:

TRIGGER: a new client is created in Stripe.

ACTION: use Outlook to send an email to the client created in Stripe.

ACTION: set a timer for fifteen days.

ACTION: use Outlook to send an email to the client created in Stripe.

You just saved time (fifteen minutes per occurrence) and made more money (50 percent better customer retention).

For example, a business we worked with had a month-to-month subscription-based product that reaches beginner entrepreneurs. They discovered that 50 percent of people who used the free trial would pay them before canceling the subscription. Of those who paid them, 50 percent would cancel after month one. But, if a customer was with them for four months, they knew their lifetime value would increase over 10X. We set out to increase the number of clients who stayed with them for four months.

We started using tools like Zapier to send engaging emails on a drip the moment they signed up for the service. Through the trial, clients heard from us consistently a few days per week, and at least once per week for the first ninety days. Our customer retention went through the roof. Almost all this work was done using automated tools.

These automations are available now and require no code be written. Anyone, even the most non-technical employees at your company, can automate tasks today.

Example: Recurring Reminder Messages

Situation

You're a bookkeeper, and every month you need the same documentation from your clients: bank statements and credit card statements.

Solution

Create a Zapier automation!

TRIGGER: schedule every month on the first of the month.

ACTION: use Outlook to send an email.

Customize who you want to send the email to, and the body, and you're done.

Saving ninety minutes per new client sign-up with simple automations.

Zapier automations are powerful. Like, really powerful. Once your team gets comfortable with "When this happens, then do that" automations, they can begin to string processes together.

Let's say an activity log, without including task switching penalties, looks something like this:

Task	Why	Time	1-5 Scale	# Occurrences/ Week
Sales call—got verbal agreement.	We do this every day.	5 minutes	2	2
Updated CRM to verbal agreement.	It's our SOP.	3 minutes	3	2
Prepared and sent the contract.	We had a new client today.	25 minutes	3	2
Sorted the contract once it was signed.	It's our SOP.	5 minutes	2	2
Sent email to budget coordinator to generate invoice.	It's our SOP.	5 minutes	3	2

Moved client deal to "Deal Won" in CRM.	It's our SOP.	5 minutes	2	2
Had meeting with customer success team to transfer client data.	It's our SOP.	25 minutes	1	2
Sent "welcome" email to new client.	It's our SOP.	5 minutes	3	2

Your employee gets a verbal agreement on a deal, logs it in the CRM, then, your sales employee fills out the contract and sends it to the prospect.

After the contract gets signed, your team updates the Pipedrive CRM to "Deal Won" and automatically sends the initial invoice using QuickBooks for 20 percent of the contract fee. They create a new project in our project management platform, Trello, add all the data from the CRM into the Trello card, and assign the customer success team to the project. Then, Zapier automatically sends a welcome email to schedule a kickoff meeting. This process, in total, can take over an hour, especially if there's a handoff meeting from the sales team to the customer success team.

What if you could automate the first part of the process?

TRIGGER: the Pipedrive CRM is updated to "Verbal Agreement."

ACTION: fill out the contract in DocuSign.

ACTION: send the contract to the primary contact in the CRM.

Your team just saved over a half hour because they didn't have to fill out and send the contract. They created one template contract and had the computer fill out the details using the information from the CRM. Even more exciting, we can automate the second part of the process as well, beginning with when the contract gets signed.

TRIGGER: a new contract is signed in DocuSign.

ACTION: create and send an invoice in QuickBooks.

ACTION: update the deal in our Pipedrive CRM to "Deal Won."

ACTION: create a new Trello card, add all the client's information, and assign our customer success team.

ACTION: use Outlook to send a welcome email and schedule a kickoff meeting.

Now let's say you've discovered that your customer retention rate increases by 50 percent when you send a "just thinking about you" email 15 days later...

Task	Why	Time	1-5 Scale	# Occurrences/ Week
Sent "thinking about you" email to new client.	It helps us increase retention.	5 minutes	1	3

TRIGGER: a new contract is signed in DocuSign.

ACTION: update the deal in our Pipedrive CRM to "Deal Won."

ACTION: create and send an invoice in QuickBooks.

ACTION: create a new Trello card, add all the client's information, and assign our customer success team.

ACTION: use Outlook to send a welcome email and schedule a kickoff meeting.

ACTION: set a timer for fifteen days.

ACTION: send a "thinking about you" email.

Feed a Billion

In many of the poorest parts of the world, girls are trafficked because they are hungry. It's an unbelievably sad reality, and it's a reality, thankfully, that is going away thanks to charities like Feed a Billion.

Feed a Billion was at a crossroads. They needed all their money to go to the cause because every time a girl is fed, she's less likely to be trafficked, but they also needed to expand their impact.

I'd met the founder, AJ Jain, at a conference and immediately fell in love with the mission. He mentioned that Feed a Billion's greatest need was expanding their digital presence and getting more people to know about them.

We determined that we would start by simply increasing their presence on social media.

We created a spreadsheet that housed all our data. We put the date and time we wanted the content posted, the copy, and the image or video. This way, we could spend one hour per week creating content, and automation would post the content for us. It would create more reliability and consistency, and since we were focusing all our energy just on creating content, we could post more engaging content.

In the end, we set up automation to manage all social media posting.

We used a Google Sheet with four columns:

- ▶ Copy

- ▶ Image/Video (this was a link to an image or video)

- ▶ Date to post

- ▶ Time to post

TRIGGER: a new row is added to a Google Sheet (this means we added new content into the queue).

ACTION: delay until the date and time specified in the row (this makes the automation wait until the time we specified).

ACTION: post to Facebook.

ACTION: pin to Pinterest.

ACTION: send an email (this email contained all the content that needed to go on Instagram).

Instagram didn't allow the automations to post content, so we had to manually post it ourselves. This was easy because we copied and pasted the content directly from the email.

Every time the automation ran, we'd post a new Facebook post and Pinterest pin, and we'd copy and paste the Instagram content into the app. We could've tweeted, too, but they didn't have Twitter.

I'm no social media expert, but with the resources we had available, this seemed like the best way to kickstart their marketing. We started at one post per day, but that was pretty easy. We upped it to two posts per day.

Sixty days later, we'd increased their number of followers by over 50 percent. All thanks to a human focus on creating great content and the consistency of AI. From there, Feed a Billion was, and is, able to tailor their social media presence per platform, and in a more human, impactful way.

The donations followed.

Your four-step process for automating tasks begins today.

First, find your experimenter. I recommend someone who loves technology and hates boring stuff.

Second, have them complete an activity log for a week. This will be enough for you and your experimenter to start evaluating where automation opportunities exist. If you can, batch tasks together that are all part of the same business process.

Zapier, IFTTT, and Microsoft Flow all do the same general thing. I talk about Zapier in this chapter because that's the tool we use, but your experimenter can choose whatever works best for them.

Third, have your automation experimenter create simple trigger/action automations in Zapier, Microsoft Flow, or IFTTT. No need to start huge; small tasks still make a difference.

Lastly, stitch those business processes together into more complex, multi-step automations that save ten minutes, thirty minutes, or more, all at once.

Rinse, and repeat.

TAKE ACTION!

1. Who could be your AI guinea pig?

2. What SaaS platforms do you use?

3. Think of your highest value employees. How much time do you think they waste on low-value tasks?

We've put dozens of examples of Zapier Zaps that we couldn't put in the book as well as explainers for how to use Zapier at ait.teammateai.com. All for free.

Chapter 4

AUTOMATION 201: CUSTOM AUTOMATIONS

T his is where the rubber meets the road.

You've given your team the liberty to create automations with tools like Zapier. They've done their activity inventories and identified the bottlenecks in the business systems. They've started to have a taste of what it's like to automate small tasks, and they're ready to have entire business processes automated.

Or they haven't had a taste of the freedom automation brings and you are starting them here.

Sometimes, beginning AI adoption within your company through custom projects provides a great example of what's possible for your employees. It gives your employees both inspiration and security to continue to automate their own jobs so they can create bigger and better value. Then, they can become self-automating.

One client had us start with a $12,000 proof-of-concept AI. It was only a six-week engagement, and at the end of six weeks, we had created such a marked impact that the project was expanded, and it's still continuing.

A truly impressive thing about this engagement, however, was our client's company culture. We built and installed AI to help them be more productive and achieve a larger overall output. Once the team saw how incredible it was to have AI as their teammate, they started creating their own automations.

Not only did they come back with other AI projects that weren't associated with the initial project, but in looking at the company Zapier account, they had over one hundred automations running at various times. Each automation saved a member of the team five minutes here and ten minutes there. The company's profitability has increased rapidly each year since they started using AI.

This chapter will give you the formula for automating any business process in your unique world. Maybe you're looking to serve your existing customers 5X faster, publish 5X more content, or acquire 5X more customers. Maybe you want to forecast 200 percent more accurately or increase teamwork and operational efficiency by 50 percent.

Where do you start?

There are two places to begin. The first is the activity log. Have a process review team look at each team member's activity logs and group relevant tasks for each process. Average the satisfaction scores of the activities. The logs that take the most time and have the lowest satisfaction scores should be on your priority list.

Then, determine a best case/worst case ROI opportunity for each activity on your priority list. *How many hours per year will each potential automation save your team? How much money could the new automation make?*

Start with whichever opportunity will have the biggest impact with the lowest risk.

If you know what the primary bottleneck process is, still complete the exercise of determining the best/worst case ROI, but move faster to build an implementation team.

Your next step is solution exploration.

Solution Exploration

Begin by hiring a solution designer on a two-month contract with an option for more. This individual is your right-hand person throughout this particular project. They report directly to the CEO and leadership, and they are responsible for project success.

It's important that the responsibility of this project doesn't fall on an existing member of your team. Your team is already swamped with work. By virtue of your company's success, they have plenty of tasks to fill their workweeks. Adding an AI project to their plate means it won't get time dedicated to it, and more importantly, because it's not their area of expertise, you may be compromising the project's probability of success.

Some companies have been successful at repurposing their existing team to lead AI adoption in the workplace. Those employees had a sole focus of AI. In companies where employees were part-time AI and part-time their regular job, those companies either failed at AI adoption or endured too much pain in the process, or both.

The employees currently doing the work that you're looking to automate are your subject matter experts (SMEs). In a series of meetings, you, your leadership, and your SMEs will want to walk your solution designer through the automation opportunity at a high level while gradually moving toward the low-level processes.

The goal of solution exploration is to determine if AI is a suitable option to solve your problem. If it is, this phase's deliverable is a complete process map of what will be automated. It should look strikingly like the standard operating procedure of the process but should also include bullet points for when you'd like AI to do the work, and when you'd like a human to do the work, as well as the difference in time/revenue/saved expenses from start to finish between now and when the AI is implemented.

Solution Viability

Assuming you have your process map deliverable and you've identified the difference in your key metrics, now it's time to see if building the solution is even feasible. This is still up to the solution designer, possibly in consultation with an app developer. The key deliverable is a technical document of exactly how you'll accomplish the tasks in the process map. Your AI team should be working on this relatively solo, with only brief consultation from you when they have questions.

Upon deliverability, have your design team come back to you with an estimation of the number of development hours it'll take to complete the project, as well as the percentage of likelihood the project can be completed according to your specifications.

While you may not understand the technical document presented, you will understand the number of development hours they project and the percentage of likelihood it can be completed according to your exact requirements.

Any percentage likelihood under 90 percent is suspect. Most likelihoods should be between 95 percent and 100 percent.

Everyone will have their own scale for what 90 percent means, but if you're confused, you can ask the following questions:

1. *What about this project makes you not 100-percent confident?*

2. *What could we do to make you 100-percent confident?*

3. *What are the biggest surprises you aren't expecting?*

4. *What are the critical components of this project for it to be successful?*

These questions will get at all the risks in the project. You haven't invested much money at this point, and I would consider risk assessment to be key.

Your solution designer should be able to provide a very rough budget estimate using the solution viability deliverable, the estimated developer hours metric, and their knowledge of AI and automation resources.

Once you have these three components, you're ready for design. Once you have made a preliminary decision on design, you can hire.

Value-to-me budgeting

I budget AI projects as value-to-me. "How much would I pay to have the process in front of me automated?" An automation that saves your team fifteen minutes per week is far different than an automation that saves your team ninety full workdays per year.

The question I ask myself is, *"What is the upper limit of what I would be willing to pay for this?"* This, first and foremost, helps frame my commitment to solving the problem. If I wouldn't pay a lot for it, either the automation should be done in-house using Zapier or it shouldn't be completed at all.

You can always negotiate down.

If the amount you'd pay doesn't match the amount the vendor will charge, find a different vendor. If the amount you'd pay doesn't match any of the vendors you talk to, don't automate the task yet. You won't ROI on the timeline you're hoping for.

Solution Exploration & Viability in Action

A prospect came to us knowing they were swamped with boring work that was laborious, stressful, and a huge bottleneck. They had a team of six on the project, and while the leadership had a general idea of the effort involved, they couldn't help but think, "There's got to be a better way."

Their business is feast or famine. There are years where it's ultra-profitable and busy, and some where there isn't much to do. The year we were approached, they were losing clients because of slow turnaround due to too much work and not enough people. Hiring and training more employees would expose them to increased risk when the sales pipeline was empty, but they needed to increase their output.

I became their solution designer. Together, we mapped out their existing process, determined the best-case and worst-case ROI in the event the process was automated, and provided a budget estimate. We signed a contract that day.

A few weeks into the project, we sat down with their leadership team to prove that we were 100-percent certain we could automate the processes for them. Our quick proof-of-concept of the time saved was so compelling that the leadership moved five of their six employees to new opportunities effective immediately, knowing that the one person who remained in the role, with AI as their teammate, could accomplish more than the team of six, combined.

Example: Customer Handoff

Situation

Let's imagine that your primary bottleneck occurs right after your sales team closes a new deal. You need to create alignment with your customer success team, alert your finance team, and alert your operations team so that proper resource planning and business intelligence can take place.

Solution Exploration

In the case of the bottleneck right after sales closes a deal, the solution designer would map out all your processes, not just in the communication of all these teams, but in the execution of their next actions. These process maps would look strikingly similar to an activity log.

Let's imagine the following things happen, all before a kickoff meeting with the client:

- ▶ Sales meets with customer success to do an intro meeting. In this meeting is the sales rep who closed the deal, the customer success leads assigned to the project, the project manager, and a member of the operations team. This meeting takes thirty minutes.

- ▶ An email is sent to the accounting department with the signed agreement.

- ▶ The member of the operations team requests the signed agreement and begins adding data into the business intelligence platform. This person also begins resource planning and mapping timelines from a high-level perspective.

- ▸ The project manager also begins resource planning and managing timelines from a project perspective. The PM and operations individuals meet weekly for thirty minutes.

- ▸ The customer success leads begin gathering requirements.

- ▸ The operations and accounting teams set up a meeting to review the new financial projects and to verify internal project budget. This is a sixty-minute meeting.

Your solution designer envisions creating a dashboard that can automate most aspects of this process. They say, "It would work something like this:"

- ▸ When a new deal is won in your CRM, a new client is created immediately in the dashboard.

- ▸ When the agreement is uploaded, the dashboard reads the contract and extracts the payment terms, deal value, an overview of the work, the project type, and the timeline to completion.

▸ Based off the project type, the dashboard will reference your other projects (since they're all in the dashboard as well), create a preliminary project plan, and suggest resource availability. You'll be able to manually change the resources assigned to the project.

▸ Not only will the business intelligence and resource utilization metrics change based off the resources assigned to the project, but the dashboard will automatically change those metrics if you decide to experiment with other options.

▸ In the dashboard, you'll be able to see the project's budget based off project type and resource investment.

▸ The deal value and payment terms will be sent automatically in an email to the accounting team. The accounting team will also be able to access the project budget.

▸ At a higher level, all key revenue, resource utilization, timeline, and customer success metrics can be viewed at a project-, department-, product-, or company-wide level, so the entire leadership team knows where everything stands.

Solution Viability

The solution designer works with an application developer to create a high-level needs assessment.

They determine that:

- ▶ You'll need a locked-down database, at least two server instances, a load balancer, and HTTPS security. Not too intense.

- ▶ You'll need the ability for different access levels, functionality based off the job, administrators, file upload, OCR (to read the contract), the ability to create interactive graphs/charts, and the ability to send emails.

- ▶ It'll need the ability to aggregate data as well.

- ▶ It'll take at least 120 days until you're in testing.

- ▶ It all needs to be mobile-friendly.

For a project like this, a UI designer is critical, along with a full-stack developer. An infrastructure and security developer is helpful, but not critical at the early stages, although they won't need to be utilized much. Mostly to make sure the servers are locked down and to make sure the dashboard can be accessed through your domain. A neural net developer isn't expected to be needed since there are tools offered by Azure, AWS, and GCP that'll do OCR for you, and interactive visualizations shouldn't need a special developer since you can embed tools created by AWS, Azure, and GCP, or simply embed a Tableau graph.

Budget

In the case of our customer handoff example, a project like this would cost $40,000 to start, with an increasing investment depending on additional customizations necessary.

Example: The Teammate Website

Here's an example of a challenge that I was bound and determined would be solved by AI.

I've rarely heard someone say, "I just overhauled my website, and you wouldn't believe how great an experience it was!" To be honest, I'm not sure why, but I have never had fun with websites either. Even though we build user interfaces and applications that live online as websites, marketing website projects never cease to be long, difficult, and expensive.

You can imagine my excitement when we were rebranding and needed to overhaul our website.

Situation

We need to overhaul our website with a focus on exactly who we serve, how we serve them, and our track record for success.

Solution Exploration

We spent a lot of time in this phase. Even though I'm CEO of Teammate, I'm more of a special team member. Really, my primary role is solution designer. I design solutions for our customers and ourselves.

We had lots of options.

We could use ClickFunnels, a software we use for digital sales funnels, to host our entire website. We could use WordPress. We could modify our old Wix site.

We could move to Squarespace. We could just build our own from scratch.

Then, our designer designed the site. It eliminated ClickFunnels, Wix, and Squarespace due to design limitations. We were left with WordPress and building our own from scratch.

I really, *really* didn't want to spend $20,000+ and three months on a new website project. I just wanted it done. There had to be a solution.

Solution Viability

I had heard of an AI tool called Anima App through a friend who works at a local design firm. She mentioned they'd used it, and their website listed Apple and Netflix as clients. I thought, "If it's good enough for them, it's probably good enough for me."

Solution

After spending a week learning the tool, the next week was spent taking designs to our designers and making them website-ready. With the click of a button, the tool exported all the code for the website, mobile responsive and already-SEO'd. I handed this code to my developers, who spun up a $4.00 per month server, connected the domain, and ran the code. Just like that, we have a website! You can see the website now at https://www.teammateai.com/.

Budget

A website developer would've coded upwards of $20,000 and taken ninety days. For a $40 per month subscription (that you can cancel), we got all the code we needed.

No solution designer? No problem.

We've included a sample job description at ait.teammateai.com, but if that doesn't work (or you don't want to interview), we can help! Email me at evan@teammateai.com and put "AI as your Teammate" in the subject line.

TAKE ACTION!

1. What process, if you could totally automate it, would bring the greatest transformation to your business and life?

Chapter 5

BUILD YOUR
PROJECT TEAM

With AI projects, "When in doubt, hire it out." Of course, that's easy for me to say since I run an AI company, but hear me out. Software projects, especially automation, can easily slide into one of two, or both, bad outcomes. I am here to help you be aware of, and avoid, common pitfalls.

The first bad outcome is the project that never ends. There's always "one more hurdle" to get over. I've found most of these projects have the wrong people doing the work. These projects will end 2–3X over budget and will take way too long to complete.

The second bad outcome, and this is the worse of the two, is when an automation is built that doesn't do what's intended. Now, you're left with a bad process that is automated, so you must create a new process to fix the automation's mistakes. Instead of freeing up your team to do bigger and better things, you've freed up your team to babysit an AI.

This chapter will address how to build a project team, where to invest more, where you can cut costs, and how to utilize incentives to achieve the results you want.

As automation complexity increases, your need for AI talent increases.

Don't outsource a simple automation that saves one to ten minutes per occurrence unless it meets both of the following criteria:

1. Nobody on the team can figure it out.

2. It occurs more than five times per week.

There are sort-of-complex automations, like the ninety-minute time-saver in Chapter 6 where everything is completed in Zapier (there's no code written), but the automation has quite a bit of complexity, and it makes a pretty big impact. To determine the value I would pay, take those ninety minutes, multiply it by the number of times that automation would've run last year, and multiply that by $30.00 per hour. The dollar figure you calculate is a rough estimate of your cost for that employee doing the specific task last year.

This exercise frames my reference for how much I would be willing to pay. For Zapier-based automations, I want to return my investment in one year or less, not including new value created with the time saved.

The rules change once custom code is written. There are cloud servers, functions, and deployment. That requires the knowledge and skills of developers. There are two types of automation projects in that bucket.

The sort-of-intense automation

Type one is the automation that requires functionality Zapier doesn't have but isn't too intense. A perfect example of this is that you have a SaaS platform that *has* an API but *isn't* on Zapier. For example, a client wanted to add user-submitted content in a published blog post. The client wants to charge for the content to show up on the site. They need to collect the content and images, verify it was not spam or inappropriate, format it to become a blog post, and publish the content.

This is a relatively simple automation; there are two ways to perform it. The development team can use Zapier to connect a TypeForm (SaaS platform) to an AWS database, which then runs a Lambda function and sends all the data to the website's CMS to publish the content as a blog post. Or the team, and this is what we did, can launch a quick AWS server, connect it to their URL as a subdomain, spin up a user interface with a data intake form that includes photo upload in a Flask app, save all that data to a database, and then send the data to the client's CMS to publish it as a blog post using the API that's not in Zapier.

My guess is that most of the above didn't make any sense. That's on purpose. This is probably not something where you want to insource solution design and development, but the price for an automation like this isn't too high if outsourced properly. A project of this complexity would most likely cost less than $20,000. Relatively cheap considering the client will make $4,000 per month without lifting a finger.

Type two is a project you'd pay over $20,000 for. This is a project where you hire a team, starting with a solution designer.

What is and isn't your job?

As an entrepreneur, your job is to understand that bottlenecks exist in your business which prevent growth.

Your job is not to know the ins and outs of your data. It's not to know the low-level of how AI works. It's not to know a CNN versus an RNN versus LSTM and GAN and any other exclusive language thrown around in the AI community. Your job is not to know how you'll deploy the software, how the software will be written, or even what a neural net is.

Your job, at a more fundamental level, is to understand that your future growth is predicated around using your existing team to create vastly more creative value faster, easier, cheaper, and bigger than anyone else in your industry. AI is the fastest, easiest, and cheapest way to do so.

It's your COO's job to know what the bottleneck is. If you're the CEO and COO, that would be your job too.

You will have a core team of subject matter experts. It is that core team's role to know the details inside of the bottleneck. They may not be able to identify the issue, but they can repeat the process over and over.

It's your AI project team's job to, in turn, make the AI a reality.

There are two methods for building your AI dream team. The first is the done-for-you option, the second is the done-by-you option.

Method 1: Hiring a product development company

Companies like Teammate AI will take care of everything for you. We design, develop, test, deploy, and scale. We create the AI algorithms and maintain them, scale your server capacity, and handle cybersecurity. If you decide you want to turn your newfound AI capability into a new business unit, we even turn it into a SaaS company with you.

Our process is straightforward. We start by coaching leadership teams and finding opportunities, and then we serve as the product development team. Then, if the client wishes, we turn the new AI product into a revenue-generating business unit.

Coaching

Most important is the coaching phase. This is where the product development company learns who you are, your dangers, opportunities, and strengths.

This is where we will help you design three things:

1. Your future

2. Your present

3. Your primary obstacles

We start with your future. *In what ways do you want your future to be bigger and better than your past? How do you want to expand your impact and capabilities? What's your vision for your company and your new levels of growth?*

Once we have clarity on that, we can discuss the present. *What are your current obstacles? What's preventing you from already being at your future destination?*

Knowing the general pain that the problem causes is typically pretty easy. It's the pain you feel right now. To make sure we automate the right processes the right way the first time, designing the solution means designing the problem.

Before we design your solution, we want to design your problem, and yes, your problem can be designed. In an AI world, we want to frame the problem so that the problem is solved once-and-for-all. This means that you, the end user, and client, never have to touch it again. Here, we look at your activity logs, processes, bottlenecks, and frustrations to determine which aspects of your problems take priority. We determine critical success factors, or things that must work for the project to be a success. We determine KPIs, and we will determine areas with the highest risk of failure.

If you already know the problems that need to be solved first, great. If you don't, we will help.

Next, we design the solutions that best fit your business. We talk about what's possible and our confidence to get the job done on time and within budget.

We work with you to answer questions such as: *What will your team's new workflow look like? What new freedoms will exist after? What are the hurdles we need to overcome? How will your team be able to leverage the new capability?*

Developing

If everyone decides to move forward with the AI project, we can develop the solution in consultation with your subject matter experts and your end users. Your primary role as CEO is providing leadership, approving visual design, functionality, and testing the software.

We release incremental product versions along the way so your team can begin to use and feel the changes coming with the AI.

Once we release the full solution, we scale the solution for you and make sure it works long into the future.

Budgeting for a 100-percent custom solution can go through an RFP process, or if you hire a company you trust, then they'll be able to present the investment options to you. Our most expensive projects have topped $500,000, and our least expensive have been as small as $25,000. With companies like ours, if you'd like to only gain clarity with coaching and product design, you can do that. You can then hire an implementation team separately. This drastically lowers the cost to an agency, but you're managing implementation. That is the YOYO method.

Method 2:
YOYO (You're on your own)

With method two, the budget and product quality are what you make it. In this section, I've included my recommendation for key hires and their responsibilities, but the most important person is the solution designer. This is your right-hand person and the individual responsible for project success.

Solution Designer

A solution designer is an individual who speaks the business language *and* the technical language. They know what the limits of AI are, they can create and present solutions to your problems, and they know what resources to bring on to accomplish the task at hand. Most importantly, they can give you a ballpark range of the investment required to get the job done. They are your right-hand person throughout the project.

If you're familiar with the software project space, the solution designer would be someone with the communication skills and technical knowledge of a business analyst with the design capabilities of a product designer.

A solution designer is the person you want to run the entire project, including making hires for talent. At minimum, they need to hire the following individuals:

1. Project manager

2. Data cleaner/validator(s)

3. Full-stack application developer(s)

4. Deep Learning/Machine Learning developer(s)

5. QA/Tester(s)

6. Graphic design/app design

At minimum, you, as the client, need to provide the following resources from your team:

1. Subject matter experts

2. End users

3. Project managers including setting a budget

4. Leadership buy-in

I recommend incentivizing the solution designer with a bonus based on completing the project under budget and ahead of schedule, with a special emphasis on the fact that the incentive will not be distributed until six months after project completion to ensure quality.

The solution designer generally saves you money because the first role they typically hire is the data cleaner and validator.

Data Cleaner and Validator

The data cleaner and validator's entire job is to make sure any data used for an AI algorithm is:

1. Representative of your real life (or is your real-life data)

2. As unbiased as possible

This is often a short-term position, and you only need to make this hire if you're using internal-only data. This is not someone you'd keep on for the entire project because, once the data looks good, the data looks good.

If you aren't using internal data, you don't need this hire because you can purchase data from a data vendor. Most of the time, purchased data costs less than $100.00 per month, and you can use it to build your algorithms. Your solution designer is responsible for knowing if you need to purchase data and where to purchase it from.

Hiring for data validation may seem like an unnecessary expense that an administrative assistant can handle, but this person makes or breaks projects. For reference, a complex machine vision algorithm we just built took thirty hours of developer time. Of those thirty hours, more than two-thirds of the time was spent just preparing the data. In a project where a client chose to prepare their own data and present it to us, it required an additional investment of about 20 percent. This position will save you *a lot* of money.

Bad data is the most common reason why an AI needs a babysitter, even after you invested lots of money to develop it. Additionally, if you don't hire this individual and the responsibility rests on the AI developer to do this data cleaning and validation, that is a very expensive mistake.

Application Developer

AI is like the brain. The brain understands data and makes decisions, but without a body, it's not useful. The application developer builds the "body."

This person or team does your infrastructure, scaling, user interface, database, buttons, security, deployment (making it visible on the internet), and overall usability. I consider this everything-but-the-AI.

Servers and infrastructure used to be expensive and difficult. That used to take an entire person or an entire team. This individual can spin up servers on AWS, Azure, or Google Cloud in a matter of minutes, and they can scale with the full power of a warehouse, if you need them to. Remember *AlphaGo* from Chapter 1? That entire program was run off AI, running on a laptop connected to Google Cloud.

This type of developer is much cheaper, but they will bill far more hours.

Your solution designer will probably hire this person before the ML/DL developer so that they can start building a project plan together.

Machine Learning/Deep Learning Developer

ML/DL developers are expensive and niche. What's that mean to you? Limit their scope.

Your solution designer may want to bring on an AI developer to also be the application developer on the project. I do not recommend that.

You'll be overspending on most of the code. Most letter-of-the-law AI is relatively simple code combined with lots of data. Most all the other code can be written by a full-stack application developer at a fraction of the price of an ML/DL developer.

Your ML/DL developer should be creating, training, testing, productionalizing, and maintaining your neural nets and that's it. They should be the ones who know which packages to use, how to set up the model, eliminate loss, and optimize the speed.

This person is a very, very valuable person, but I cannot emphasize this enough: limit their scope.

Your ML/DL developer may tell you that they need to build the rest of the product so it "works properly." Please allow me to assure you, that's not true. Our ML/DL developers and our application developers typically integrate the AI into the application in one thirty-minute meeting.

What I mean is, the person who builds the AI doesn't need to build the rest of the product. The two just need to talk to each other to connect the brain and the body together. If the person who builds the brain builds the rest of the product, you'll certainly overspend and possibly have a mediocre automation across the board.

QA/Testing

This person is often part-time and will appear in the mix once user acceptance testing has begun. They only need to test when there's a new release, and they can both create and follow test scripts. I'd consider this to be the extent of their duties.

Graphic Design/App Design

Most of the time, I recommend bringing in a graphic designer to make sure that the application is designed properly. This will allow you to have a visually appealing application for automation and, secondly, allow your solution designer and your team to think through the functionality of the application.

This person is on the front-end of the project. They can be used in a consultative capacity, for UX, UI, and to ask questions you may not have thought of, and their end-deliverable is an application wireframe.

Project Manager

Unless your solution designer is also a very organized individual, I recommend a software project manager. This is the only position I'd consider porting from your core team over to this project.

Your AI Project Team's Responsibility

Your AI project team's responsibility is to manage the project and deliver the solution. It's not your responsibility to demand certain project methodologies, deployment strategies, and technical specifications unless you've got an IT team working with your AI project team.

There's a difference between software that works and software that works for your business. You can expect that your subject matter experts will test the solution. This testing will ensure the solution solves your specific use case.

As entrepreneur and founder, your job is to begin thinking about your future teamwork.

Example: Quality Assurance

Situation

You're an insurance adjuster, engineering consultant, general contractor, or designer. You've got too much work on your plate and not enough human resources to do QA on all the different components of your projects. You find that there are certain fixtures that are often installed improperly, leading to their needing replacement earlier than expected.

You're losing clients to your competitors because you can't fulfill the inspections and documentation fast enough. You can't find enough inspectors to do the job, and you'd really like to not hire more inspectors, anyway, because they're expensive, but you need to have them. Beyond that, one of your inspectors is nearing retirement age.

Where do you start?

Your inspectors' activity inventories show that they spend too much time going from inspection site to inspection site. They also spend way too much time taking photos.

Solution Exploration

You discuss the opportunity of having non-trained inspectors go out and take photos. This would be much cheaper than your inspectors' time driving, and they would upload the photos to Dropbox where your inspectors can review them and provide feedback.

You also discuss the opportunity to have a mobile app built for your photographers which automatically takes a photo of the window when it sees that there's damage.

Solution Viability

The second option, only taking a photo when the mobile app sees damage, is sleek, but it's high-risk. What if the AI is wrong?

There's no backup plan with that.

The first option of having non-trained inspectors taking photos of every window is interesting. At least, then, you have a backup plan if the mobile app fails. You can have your inspection team at the office, or behind a computer, verifying that the images show accuracy, and you can pay much cheaper labor to take the photos and upload them.

There's no AI in this process yet, but if you can have AI in the mobile app, you can have it here too. You decide to hire a solution designer to look at the project further.

Solution Designer

Your solution designer sees that you can have an AI do the first pass to look at all the images. Instead of your inspectors looking at every one, especially when you know that almost all of them will look good, the AI does the first pass. Anything the AI isn't sure about goes to the inspector, and from there, any sort of damage or QA issue is detected manually.

Project Team

In this case, a sophisticated project team would be required.

You would need:

- ▶ A solution designer

- ▶ A data cleaner (to gather and label old images so the neural net developer can train the AI)

- ▶ A full-stack developer (to build the body of the application)

- ▶ A neural net developer (to do machine vision on the images)

- ▶ A project manager

You would also need to make your inspectors and end-users available to test the software.

Budget

With only these specifications, the budget for an application like this would start at $20,000.

Measuring ROI

ROI is measured in "time to inspect and verify," and you expect you can reduce that time by 50 percent or more. You'll save client relationships and be less stressed at the same time. You decide to hire a team and move forward with the project.

Immediate Impact

Your inspectors are more efficient than ever before. You have marginal added expense in photographers, but you're getting reports and projects out so much faster that you hardly see any impact. You're saving client relationships, and you and your team are far less stressed than before.

Long-Term Impact

The inspector nearing retirement age retires. Instead of spending time and cash training a new inspector, your team is so much more efficient that consolidating work is easy.

Inspection issues have become an afterthought. Now, you have an inspection arm of your business which subcontracts from your competitors. You realize that your competitors have the same problems you do, and so now you can sell the services to them. For anything that you have photographers trained on, you send them to do the same process you do for yourself. For anything that your photographers aren't trained on, you send your inspectors, who used to do that work every day, to the inspection site. Now, for you, your photographers and your inspectors have gone from a "necessary expense" to a billable resource. For them, they have more variety in their workdays and feel like every day brings new challenges.

For you, it's almost all profit. For them, it's a weight lifted off their shoulders.

Example: Sales Activity Tracking & Account Executive Management

Situation

Your sales manager or general manager would like to track account executive activity for job performance. Your performance reviews right now are based solely on reaching a quota, but you'd like to track more leading indicators.

Solution Exploration

Your primary option is to track activities in your CRM with the mindset of "If it's not in the CRM, it didn't happen." This is a good starting place, although there are change management issues associated with it.

You use a CRM that's integrated with Zapier, but your sales team is busy, and a Zapier subscription could get expensive, fast. Your immediate move is to hire a solution designer.

Your solution designer presents you with three options:

1. Use the API from your CRM to store activity data in Airtable and let Airtable make the graphs.

2. Use the API from your CRM to store activity data in a database and send it to Tableau.

3. Use the API from your CRM to store activity data in a Google Sheet.

The only real difference is where the data is stored. Considering your sales team would quickly exhaust a Zapier subscription, you remove option three. Nobody on your team knows Airtable well enough, so that's out. You're left with storing data in a database and using Tableau.

Solution Viability

This is relatively common. While it requires developer investment, it's very doable.

Solution Designer

Hired. It's a ninety-day engagement.

Immediate Impact

It's so freeing to see each sales rep's activities every week. Tableau is easy to use, and sales management is way easier.

Top performing sales reps and underperforming sales reps are now measured by more metrics than just quota, and your sales manager starts tweaking aspects of your territories, prospecting, and sales funnel to optimize close rates.

Long-Term Impact

You can hire, fire, promote, and support employees based off more than just one number. It becomes such a huge component to your performance reviews that your leadership starts looking for ways to track activities across the business. The business, over time, becomes more and more data-driven and predictable, leaving you with a self-managing company.

TAKE ACTION!

1. What do you know now that you didn't know before?

2. What hesitations might your team have about AI?

3. What pushback might you get from leadership?

Chapter 6

YOUR TEAM'S BIGGER FUTURE AFTER AI

Once your AI is running properly and creativity spaces have opened, one question looms: what do you do *next*?

How do you repurpose your team?

I fundamentally believe that the role of AI is to free up your team to do more fascinating, motivating, and creative work. AI serves as an always-on teammate for your team.

The role of a team member

I believe there are three types of employees:

1. Anchors: employees that hold the business back.

2. Maintainers: employees that maintain the business as it is.

3. Growers: employees that drive growth and positive progress in the business.

Businesses need both Maintainers and Growers. To get a truly accurate picture of the three types of employees, we need to subset them out.

Anchors

Employees that hold the business back are wrong-fit employees. You know who they are, they know that you know who they are, and neither party is happy in the business arrangement, but the inconvenience of parting ways doesn't outweigh the inconvenience of finding someone new.

Maintainers

There are two types of maintainers. The first group of maintainers are truly wired for habit. These people are your trusted employees who rarely, if ever, make a mistake. They double- and triple-check their work, and if everything was in a crash-and-burn state, you'd trust them to help navigate the situation first. These people also know the skeletons in the closet, the weaknesses in the products and systems, and the ways around them.

The other group of maintainers are actually growers, but they're stuck in maintainer roles. These people know how processes and products can be improved and often have ideas for adjacent opportunities that can be hugely profitable. These people will create the AI fan club inside of your business because they see it as an opportunity to move into a growth-oriented role.

Pro tip: your best maintainers are your subject matter experts as you're doing AI implementation.

Growers

Growers drive growth in one of two ways. The first is by creating new opportunities, and the second is by optimizing old opportunities.

Those who create new opportunities are looking at new products to release, strategies to try, and markets to enter.

Those who optimize old opportunities see a process, product, or strategy, and they squeeze out every ounce of productivity they can find.

All growers love to grow.

Time saves time saves time.

Every time a task is automated, a new creativity space opens. *A creativity space is the moment in time when a person would've done a task, and now they don't have to because the AI is responsible for it.* Every time you hired a new person to do a job you were previously doing, you experienced the magic of a creativity space.

Without new creativity spaces, new value creation opportunities have a difficult time showing themselves, but in a world where AI is your teammate, every instance an automation runs, a new creativity space opens. This forms a positive feedback loop, where each time a task is automated, a creativity space is created.

At first, the product of the creativity spaces may be new automations.

At some point, and it usually comes when a member of your team has automated five hours per week, the creativity space asks a new question. Not: *what else can be automated?* Instead, the question is: *what new things can I be doing?*

In this moment, that team member's future is bigger than their past.

When a teammate asks that question, their future value creation exceeds their past. Their goals and trajectory exceed what they thought possible, relative to the timeline they were expecting.

Why? Because your company's value creation is the sum of the value creation of all members of your team. When one member of your team can drive radically bigger value, your company's value creation increases.

Then, AI becomes more widely adopted in the company. Each member of your team has five, ten, or maybe even twenty hours automated. In total, over 50 percent of tasks inside of your core business are automated, and AI is the new backbone of your business.

Imagine a member of your team leaves. That's okay! Your existing processes are being completed by AI. No training, no downtime. No distractions or shared responsibilities. You hire for the new role that the former employee created, and you continue progressing into the future.

While AI is making sure the lights stay on in the present, your existing team is propelling your business forward. This accelerates your 10X growth.

Let's take it a step further. Let's assume your team has grown the business 10X. Is their future still bigger than their past? Absolutely! So they start using AI as their teammate again.

They'll start with the activity log, which will lead to Zapier automations that free up five to ten minutes per week. Over time, more custom automations will be built. They'll free up ten to twenty hours. The maintainers maintain, the growers grow, and the cycle repeats itself. Except with each iteration, your company and your impact grows faster, easier, and bigger.

Your bigger future with AI does not need to be competing with companies in Silicon Valley. It's not starting a new internet business or becoming the next Steve Jobs or Elon Musk. Your bigger future with AI is by using AI as your teammate in your existing business and allowing your existing team to create 10X growth.

AI is not the replacement of humans. AI is your *teammate*.

Your teamwork of the future.

Your growers will be gung-ho about automation, efficiencies, and getting more done in less time. These people oftentimes overcommit themselves anyway, so AI is a welcomed relief.

As they start to have more and more free time, they will look for new opportunities to create value inside the company. Most times, these employees treat their careers entrepreneurially. They want to grow as fast and big as they can, but inside the safety of a job. This should be music to your ears.

Growers often want to take on new initiatives. I recommend asking them for their suggestions. I can almost guarantee they know the lowest-hanging fruit for new value creation.

Since they have more time, they can make progress faster. Since they're working on new forms of value creation, they're more fascinated and motivated than ever before.

Your maintainers fill in key gaps that the AI hasn't filled in yet. You can consolidate job responsibilities to your maintainers and away from growers as you see fit, and you can restructure your teamwork to be focused on "existing opportunities" (maintainer-work) and "future opportunities" (grower-work). Since maintainers want to follow established processes, they will relish the opportunity to have more ownership over existing processes. Since growers want to push the envelope of their and your capabilities, they'll relish the opportunity to hand over some of their process-oriented job responsibilities to maintainers.

Everyone will feel like they got a promotion.

AI as your company backbone.

Over time, AI and automation will augment or replace most processes. Most businesses start with small tasks and expand over a few years. From our experience, this is a good thing for your maintainers because it keeps them from shock.

Right around the time the new opportunities your growers created come to fruition they need help from...your maintainers! Your growers have transformed new, prospective opportunities into solid, profitable opportunities that could use some stability.

Because AI supports your maintainers in your core business, your maintainers can help the growers stabilize their new initiatives. As your maintainers get busier, the need for automation will show itself. It'll be time to create a new activity log and begin automating processes again!

Zapier automations will become custom automations. Your new opportunities can leverage AI as their teammate to see efficiency improvements. More automation will create more creativity spaces, and more creativity spaces will create more opportunities for your growers.

AI, as your company backbone, helps your team. It means that your team can elevate themselves to new levels of fascination and motivation. As your company grows, each of your employees grows.

TAKE ACTION!

1. What new opportunity have I wanted to capitalize on but couldn't because we were too busy?

Conclusion

In the two months following Lee Sedol's tournament against *AlphaGo*, where he lost four games to one, he won every tournament match he played.

The DeepMind team had set their sights on a new challenge. They were going to build a new AI to play *Go*, but only teach it by playing against *itself*. This means that this new AI would learn *Go* not by playing against a human, but by playing against an AI.

Just like with Atari *Breakout*, the new AI, called *AlphaGo Zero*, was only taught using what was on the screen, and it was told to "maximize the probability of winning."

After just three days of learning, the DeepMind team pitted *AlphaGo Zero* against *AlphaGo*, the algorithm which had defeated world champion Lee Sedol four games to one.

AlphaGo Zero's win record against *AlphaGo*? One hundred games to zero.

What if your business moved at that speed? What if your business had so much technology leverage that the limiting factor to your growth was your creativity?

What new businesses would you create? What new people would you serve?

What opportunities would that open for the rest of your team?

Transformations, at some level, always involve adding new colleagues and capabilities into your business and your world. AI gives you the capabilities to do what humans are doing now but shouldn't be.

Humans are hired to do tasks. The sum of those tasks becomes their output, and that's why you pay them, but what if we could increase the value of those tasks? What if we could increase their output while decreasing the number of tasks they perform?

Whether you're building a project team and embarking on a high-impact, high-budget custom AI or building low-budget Zapier Zaps, all automation creates new time for your employees. It creates opportunities for them to think deeper and think different. It allows them to focus less on tasks that anyone, or anything, can do and more on tasks only they can do.

Is the key for transforming your business making humans more efficient, or is it changing the value those humans create?

Maybe, as Henry Ford liked to say, the solution isn't "faster horses." Maybe the way to grow your business, your impact, and your employee's futures is by having AI handle the repetitive aspects of your business and by rethinking the role of the employee. Maybe, instead of an employee's role being to maintain the current operations of your business, their role can be taking on new challenges, creating new opportunities, and serving new people.

At the end of the day, isn't every entrepreneur's dream to have a company that's always growing, yet predictable?

Further Resources

If anything in this book is confusing, if any of it is too technical and you'd like a higher-level explanation, or if there are any gaps in knowledge you find, please email me at evan@team mateai.com. Also, feel free to email me and just say "Hello." In the subject line, put "AI as your Teammate."

On ait.teammateai.com we've included lots of specific information about AI, along with further resources, including:

▶ videos of DeepMind's AI playing *Brick Breaker*;

▶ a glossary of AI terms and what you should think when you hear them;

▶ a solution designer job description;

- ▸ a write-up of $0.00 marginal cost businesses *and just how great they are*;

- ▸ different types of data and how they can be used;

- ▸ video lessons about how you can make your own Zapier Zaps;

- ▸ Zapier Zaps we didn't put in the book, but we love to use;

- ▸ tools for how anyone in your organization can identify opportunities for AI;

- ▸ and much more!

CPSIA information can be obtained
at www.ICGtesting.com
Printed in the USA
LVHW090724071221
705350LV00043B/198/J